Dolls' Houses

Other books by Shirley Glubok:

The Art of Ancient Egypt
The Art of Lands in the Bible
The Art of Ancient Greece
The Art of the North American Indian
The Art of the Eskimo
The Art of Ancient Rome
The Art of Africa
Art and Archaeology
The Art of Ancient Peru
The Art of the Etruscans
The Art of Ancient Mexico
Knights in Armor
The Art of India
The Art of Japan
The Art of Colonial America
The Art of the Southwest Indians
The Art of the Old West
The Art of the New American Nation
The Art of the Spanish in the United States
   and Puerto Rico
The Art of China
The Art of America from Jackson to Lincoln
The Art of America in the Gilded Age
The Art of America in the Early Twentieth
   Century

The Art of America Since World War II
The Art of the Northwest Coast Indians
The Art of the Plains Indians
The Art of the Woodland Indians
The Art of Photography
The Art of the Southeastern Indians
The Art of the Vikings
The Art of the Comic Strip
The Fall of the Aztecs
The Fall of the Incas
Discovering Tut-Ankh-Amen's Tomb
Discovering the Royal Tombs at Ur
Digging in Assyria
Home and Child Life in Colonial Days
Dolls Dolls Dolls
The Art of Egypt under the Pharaohs

With Alfred Tamarin:

Ancient Indians of the Southwest
Voyaging to Cathay: Americans in the China Trade
Olympic Games in Ancient Greece
The Mummy of Ramose: The Life and Death of an Ancient
   Egyptian Nobleman

Shirley Glubok

DOLLS' HOUSES

Life in Miniature

Harper & Row, Publishers

Acknowledgments

The author gratefully acknowledges the assistance of: ELIZABETH M. DONOGHUE, Curator of Dolls, Wenham Historical Association and Museum, Inc., Wenham, Mass.; JORŪNN FOSSBERG, Head Curator, Norsk Folkemuseum, Oslo, Norway; HANNE GANZHORN, Museum Conservateur, Legoland A/S, Billund, Denmark; CAROLINE GOODFELLOW, Research Assistant, Bethnal Green Museum of Childhood, Victoria and Albert Museum, London, England; GEORGE HUTZLER; FLORA GILL JACOBS, Director, The Washington Dolls' House and Toy Museum, Washington, D.C.; DR. BÉATRICE JANSEN, Head, Department of Applied Art, and Vice-Director, Haags Gemeentemuseum, The Hague, Netherlands; JOHN NOBLE, Curator of the Toy Collection, Museum of the City of New York; ESTHER DOANE OSMAN, Old Newbury Historical Society, Newburyport, Mass.; THALE RIISÖEN, Curator, Vestlandske Kunstindustriemuseum, Bergen, Norway; DR. LEONIE VON WILCKENS, Curator, Germanisches Nationalmuseum, Nuremberg, West Germany; *and especially the helpful cooperation of:* CLARE LE CORBEILLER, Associate Curator, European Sculpture and Decorative Arts, The Metropolitan Museum of Art, New York, N.Y.; MARILYN JOHNSON, Associate Curator, American Wing, The Metropolitan Museum of Art, New York, N.Y.; EDWARDA ZETTELER, Assistant Curator, Frans Halsmuseum—De Hallen, Haarlem, Netherlands.

Library of Congress Cataloging in Publication Data
Glubok, Shirley.
 Dolls' houses.

 Summary: Presents twenty-six miniature historic houses
reflecting the arts and cultures of various times and
places, from the seventeenth century to the present.
 1. Doll-houses—Juvenile literature. [1. Dollhouses.
2. Miniature objects] I. Title.
NK4893.G56 1984   745.592′3′094   77–25663
ISBN 0-06-022016-3   ISBN 0-06-022017-1 (lib. bdg.)

Designed by Constance Fogler
1 2 3 4 5 6 7 8 9 10

Dolls' Houses

For those who love tiny things, there is nothing as fascinating as dolls' houses. They lead us into a private world of faraway places and times long past, for these little homes are history in miniature. Their styles record the architecture of their time, and their furnishings reflect the decorative arts and social customs of the period.

The first dolls' houses were considered much too valuable for children to play with. They were wooden cabinets filled with small treasures to amuse wealthy adults. But as traditions changed, dolls' houses were used to teach young people the art of organizing and taking care of a home. To have a miniature, make-believe world of one's own that can be controlled is perfect child's play; so dolls' houses became favorite playthings for children. Today young and old alike enjoy making and playing with miniature things.

The story of dolls' houses is almost three hundred years old. The earliest ones were made in Western Europe, where the nobility and wealthy middle-class people wanted to surround themselves with objects of beauty.

In the seventeenth century the Dutch were sailing all over the world, establishing colonies and transporting foreign goods to European ports. Dutch merchants and bankers grew wealthy from foreign trade and built large, comfortable homes filled with fine furniture and works of art. They liked to collect tiny things and display them in "cabinets of curiosities." Sometimes the shelves of large wooden cupboards were divided by partitions and made into little rooms decorated in the current fashion. These cabinets filled with miniature furniture became the earliest dolls' houses.

Rijksmuseum, Amsterdam

In the late seventeenth century Petronella Dunois of Amsterdam furnished a simple Dutch cabinet that she had divided into eight rooms. The room at the left on the lowest shelf is a wine cellar. In a real house it would be underground. Wine and food were stored in the cellar, as it was the coolest place in the house. The next room is the kitchen. A woman stands beside a big open fireplace with a wide overhanging chimneypiece, where all the family's meals were cooked. Fireplaces were the only source of heat in the home and also an important source of light. The surface of this kitchen fireplace is decorated with small square tiles, miniatures of the popular Dutch tiles made in Delft. Long-handled pans, kettles, pitcher, coffeepot, teapots, cups and saucers and a variety of baskets are nearby, ready to be used for preparing dinner.

On the top shelf at the right is the nursery, where a nursemaid is watching over a baby. Next to that is the laundry room, where two laundresses are doing the family wash and drying it on a rack that hangs from the rafters in the ceiling.

Bedrooms were also used as sitting rooms, where visitors were received. When friends came to call, a fire would burn brightly in the fireplace in the great bedchamber on the second floor. Beds were big and were placed in the center of the spacious rooms of wealthy families. Mattresses were high, so a stool might be needed to climb into bed. A post at each corner of the bed supports a canopy with curtains that could be pulled all around to keep out cold drafts when the fire burned low. The fabric of the bed curtains and bedspread is also used to cover the walls. Using fabrics that matched was considered good taste.

In the drawing room, next to the bedroom, a woman is standing in front of a cupboard in which linens are stored. There were no built-in closets in seventeenth-century homes, so the Dutch used large, square storage cupboards. Sheets and tablecloths were woven of linen thread, spun from the stems of the flax plant, and even though these items today are usually made from cotton and synthetic materials, the term "linens" is still used.

The table and straight-backed chairs in this room have spiral legs, considered stylish at the time, and the walls are covered with costly imported silk cloth. Ever since Marco Polo's return from China in the thirteenth century, beautiful silks were in great demand by wealthy Europeans. Only the Chinese knew the secrets of cultivating the little worms that feed on mulberry bushes and spin lustrious silk threads, so all silk had to be imported from the Far East. Framed portraits hang on the silk-covered walls, and the ceiling is divided into sections, with pictures painted directly onto its surface.

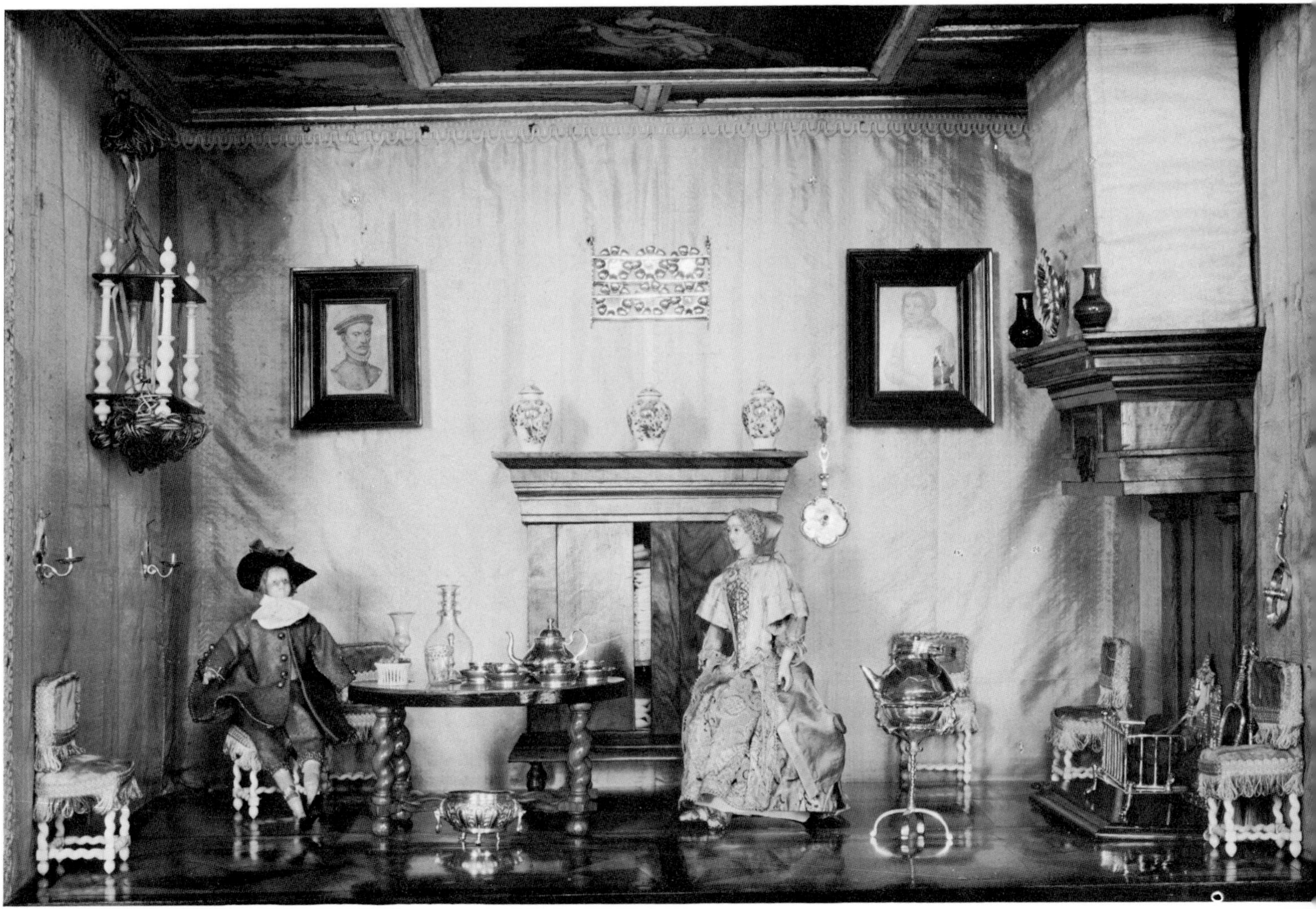

Rijksmuseum, Amsterdam

Central Museum der Gemeente Utrecht

THIS laundry room is from a Dutch cabinet that was owned by a rich tobacco merchant in the early eighteenth century. Sheets are being smoothed by the woman standing at the long table, and then dampened and ironed by the women in the foreground. Irons were heated by filling them with hot coals from the fire. After the sheets are ironed they are put into the linen press, at the right, to flatten them. Then they are stacked in a cupboard, with a neat ribbon around each pile. The laundry list, on the wall above the linen press, is used to keep count of the wash.

ANOTHER room from the same Dutch cabinet represents a storage pantry. On the top shelf are barrels of meat, salted for preservation. The shelf below contains labeled jars of rice, oats, barley, peas and beans. Under that is a rack filled with eggs. In the right foreground a mousetrap is set, ready to snap on any hungry little rodent that might try to nibble the food in this pantry. The spinning wheel in the middle of the room was used for spinning thread that was later woven into cloth and sewn into clothing for the family. All garments were made at home, from start to finish.

A maidservant, whose sleeping quarters are behind the slotted rear wall, is holding a basket of dust rags. Other baskets and a brush hang on the wall. There is even a pair of ice skates, for traveling the frozen canals of Amsterdam in winter.

Central Museum der Gemeente Utrecht

8

IN 1743 a Dutch woman named Sara Rothé, who was married to Jacob Ploos van Amstel, bought three cupboards full of miniature furnishings at an auction. Many of the furnishings had been made in the preceding century, so they were already antiques.

To display her treasures, Sara Rothé had a cabinetmaker build two cabinets, which were divided into rooms and decorated in the style of her day. Jurriaan Buttner, a well-known artist, painted decorations onto the walls and ceilings of the rooms, and he also painted little framed pictures. Sara Rothé's silversmith made additional silver for her and stamped it with his hallmark. Every master metalsmith had his own hallmark, a symbol that identifies the maker.

The first cabinet, of beautiful walnut, has three shelves, which are partitioned into nine rooms. The center section of the lowest shelf is painted to look like a formal garden, with a balustrade and stone urns in the background and a fountain with a statue in the foreground. To the right of the garden is the kitchen. One of the tiny porcelain vases on the fireplace mantel was imported from the Far East and had been one of Sara Rothé's favorite childhood playthings. Chinese porcelain had been highly prized in Europe ever since 1604, when the first big shipment arrived and was put on sale in Amsterdam. The Chinese kept the materials and manufacturing process for porcelain a carefully guarded secret. Pewter, a mixture of tin and lead, was the popular tableware before Europeans were able to make their own porcelain. The large plates on the shelves behind the glass doors are made of pewter.

One of the maidservants in the kitchen has a belt around her waist that holds a case for needles and scissors and also a case for a knife and fork. Table forks were introduced in the late seventeenth century, and it was considered good manners for people to bring their own knives and forks to meals. Before that diners had to manage mostly with their fingers.

The narrow area with the tall arched doorway in the center of the second shelf is an entrance hall. In a real house it would be reached from the street by a flight of stairs. A candle in a lantern hanging from the ceiling lights this room.

A "grandfather clock," which is actually a small gold pocket watch in a tall wooden case, tells the hour.

An interest in the wonders of nature is reflected in the landscape scenes painted on the walls of the music room, to the left of the entrance hall. The room is lit by candles in silver sconces—wall brackets—which are attached to silk ribbons that seem to be hanging from the tops of the painted trees. The host and his guest have perhaps played some music on the miniature harpsichord, flute and viola da gamba and had a game of chess, and now they are ready for a drink from the silver wine cooler on the floor in the foreground. Afterward, as the visitor leaves, he will pick up his hat and sword by the table.

Each object in the cabinet was created by a fine craftsman. The furniture was made by a cabinetmaker; the little kitchen utensils by a founder or coppersmith; the chinaware by a potter; and the paintings by an artist. Each artisan belonged to a guild, or association of craftsmen, and he was allowed to work only in his own specialty.

In homes of the noble and wealthy, a separate room might be set aside for a collection of treasures; the idea of our modern museums developed from these "collectors' rooms." Sometimes they were filled with Chinese porcelain. In this cabinet the collector's room, on the right of the entrance hall, is filled with vases made of milk glass, or white glass, which has been painted to imitate Chinese porcelain. The oval-shaped object painted with a scene, in imitation of Chinese lacquered furniture, is a tilt-top table, which folds upright when not in use. Teapots and cups and saucers are set out on two little tea tables. Merchant ships sailing all over the world collected tea, coffee and cocoa and introduced these beverages to Europeans. To fit the new drinking customs, new shapes in tables and in silverware and porcelain were developed.

A large jar on its own stand is decorated with a Japanese design. The Dutch East India Company had a monopoly on Japanese goods and shipped them all over Europe.

The chairs, which are upholstered in smooth silk, were imported from England. Framed mir-

rors, which were very expensive, are hanging on the side walls. King Louis XIV of France lined the walls of a hall in his palace at Versailles with mirrors, and it was stylish all over Europe to copy fashions from the French court. People in Amsterdam bought books with pictures of French ornaments, and those who could afford it traveled to France to see the styles firsthand. The Dutch might also import Persian or Turkish carpets for their homes, such as the one painted on this floor.

SARA ROTHÉ's second cabinet contained twelve rooms. In the laundry room, on the top floor in the center, a folding screen is painted with Japanese figures, imitating the magnificent screens that Dutch traders brought back from the Far East. A ladder leaning against the wall is handy for reaching the rafters, where clothes are hung to dry.

Visitors can gather in the elegant music room, on the third shelf at left, and listen to tunes played on the harpsichord. Windows and a lovely tall mirror reach to the ceiling.

The room to the right is the lying-in room, where the parents can receive guests who come to see the new baby. The midwife, who performed the delivery at home, is standing in front of the bed. The baby can sleep in the wicker cradle, and its diapers are kept in a basket with a silk cover. A large cupboard with Chinese porcelains on top holds neatly folded antique linen sheets, and shirts with lace collars.

A spectacular collection of miniature silver is displayed in the room on the second shelf at the left. The built-in cabinet with sliding doors reaches almost to the ceiling. Some of the silver pieces that are displayed on brackets were antique. Arnoldus van Geffen, of Amsterdam, a specialist in miniature silver, made several of the newer pieces for Sara Rothé and stamped them with his hallmark. The marble fireplace with a mirror on the overhanging chimneypiece is in the French style, and portraits of English royalty are in fancy oval frames. In the late seventeenth century a Dutch prince, William of Orange, married the English princess Mary, and he ruled England as King William III.

NEXT is a collector's room representing a doctor's study, reflecting a growing interest in medical science. Pharmaceutical pots made in Delft, jars of powder to cure diseases and small bottles of objects for scientific study stand on the shelves. One of these contains a grasshopper and a fly.

The secretary desk holds a set of books, among them *The Odyssey,* Homer's epic poem about the travels of Ulysses. The large volumes lying flat are descriptive books about Dutch towns, with tiny printed pictures. On the floor in the corner is an iron chest with a lock, which was used as a safe by the doctor, who sits in a high-backed chair, surrounded by his treasures. He is wearing a dressing gown and cap, for it was the custom for men to take off their street clothes and wigs when they came home.

The doctor was a later addition to the cabinet; originally there were no doll occupants.

SOME Dutch houses had a "best kitchen," which served as a combination dining, sitting and collector's room. The "best kitchen" in a cabinet owned by Petronella Oortman has an octagonal, or eight-sided, ceiling made to look like a skylight that would admit light into the room from above. The walls are lined with plain white square tiles. A cabinet painted with designs of flowers and leaves covers one entire side of the room. Miniature porcelains and fine glassware are lined up on all the shelves and on the fireplace mantel and even hang on hooks from the tile walls. These treasures represented Petronella Oortman's dowry, the valuable possessions she took with her when she married.

A birdcage hangs from the ceiling by the fireplace. Canaries were popular household pets and were one of the first trade items explorers brought back from South America. A wicker basket is stuffed with trash to suggest that the house is lived in. A door on the right side of the room leads to a kitchen, where dinner is cooking in a pot hanging from a chain over the open fire.

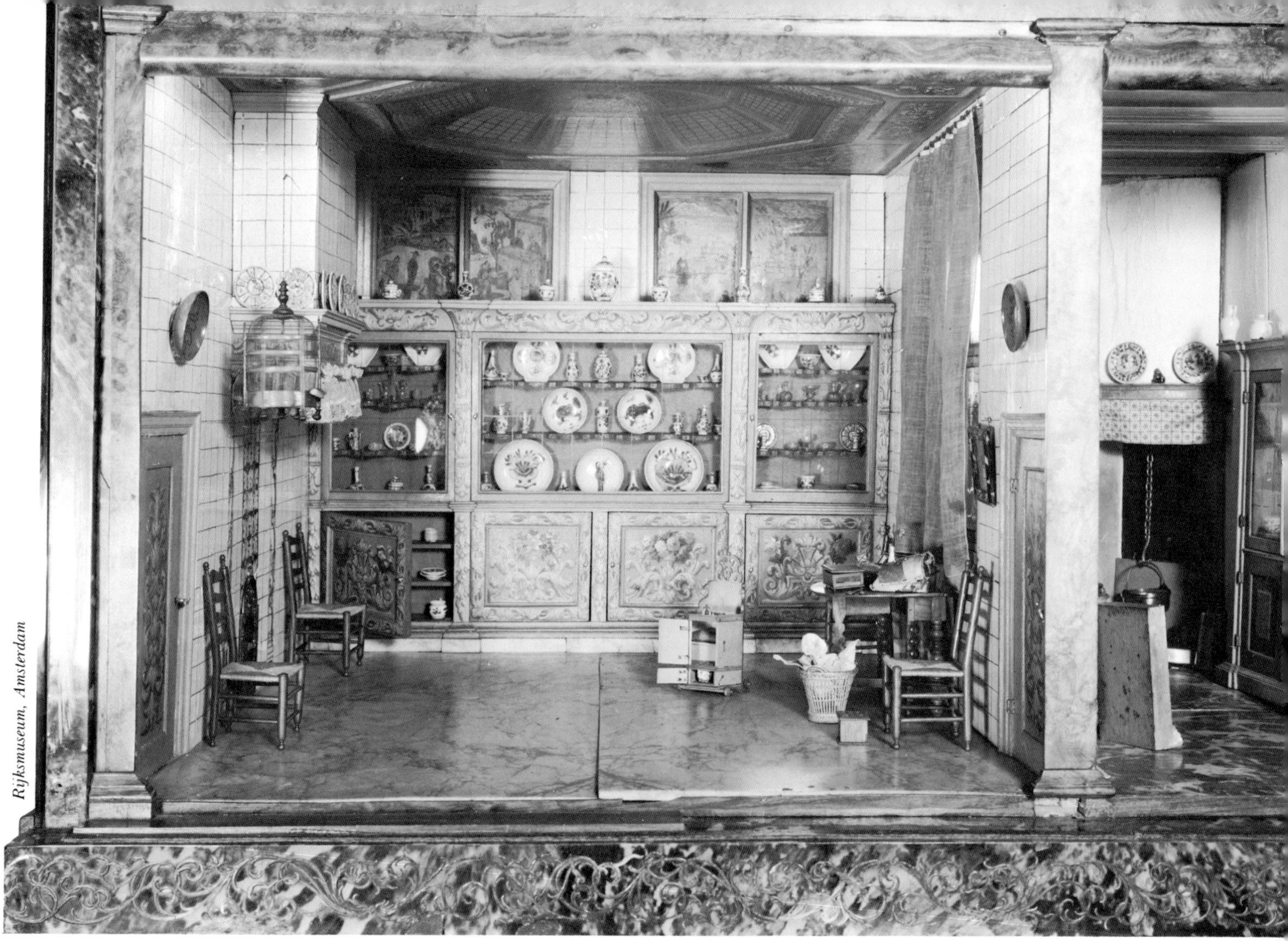

Rijksmuseum, Amsterdam

18

CABINETS filled with collections of miniatures were also popular in Scandinavia. A tall, graceful Swedish cupboard with four shelves and a paned glass door was furnished by Maria Catherina Falck in the early eighteenth century as a typical upper-class Swedish home. Most of these objects are the original ones, but some were added at a later time by descendants of Mrs. Falck. In the kitchen, along the wall on the first shelf, large pewter plates are lined up in a rack. They are actually a bit large in proportion to the furniture in the cabinet. One to twelve, or an inch to a foot, is the standard scale for dolls' house furnishings. But the fact that some objects are slightly out of proportion often adds to their charm.

The large variety of kitchen utensils includes a grater, a cutting board and a sieve. The round object with a long handle hanging on the wall is a brass warming pan. On winter nights before the family retired, a servant would fill the pan with hot coals from the fire and move it rapidly between the cold sheets to warm the beds. In the large, open fireplace at left an iron pot stands on a trivet so the food can cook slowly. To the right of the kitchen is the china room, where a set of painted dishes manufactured in Stockholm in 1746 is displayed.

The second shelf is the only one that is partitioned into rooms. At the left is a bedroom, and next to that is a sitting room, where a woman is working at a clock reel. This was used to wind thread after it had been spun on the spinning wheel, to the right. Framed portraits of important-looking people, perhaps relatives of the owner, hang on walls painted with graceful borders. The chairs are made of heavy cardboard glued together and painted gold. A handsome stove made of wood, painted to look like one covered with beautiful square tiles, reaches from floor to ceiling in the corner at right. Tall porcelain stoves on legs were a typical feature in Swedish homes.

Nordiska Museet, Stockholm

ᴖ THE third shelf is the ballroom, a perfect place for large formal parties. A checkerboard pattern on the floor imitates black and white marble. The lower part of the walls is paneled wood, and the upper part is covered with wallpaper hand painted in beautiful landscape designs. A narrow horizontal panel that projects just below the wallpaper is called the chair rail, because it protects the wall from chairs that might be shoved against it. Hanging all along the wall are mirrors with sconces for holding candles.

Another mirror hangs over the fireplace, which is painted to look like marble. Two miniature statues carved from ivory stand on the mantelpiece, and a tin fire screen in front of the fireplace prevents sparks from jumping out of the fire. The painted table at right would have been opened for dining. Later the leaves would be folded down, and the table and the elegant gilded dining chairs, upholstered with plush silk cushions, would be pushed against the wall to make room for dancing.

⫷ On the top shelf, where the walls were painted to imitate pressed leather, there is a beautiful chest of drawers. Its surface is veneered, or overlaid with a pattern of thin pieces of fine wood, and the drawers have gilt bronze drawer pulls and tiny keyholes. This chest is typical of elegant eighteenth-century Swedish furniture. The rest of the furniture in the room and the chandeliers were made in the nineteenth century.

AROUND 1730 the family of a Norwegian banker named Christopher Eege, who lived in the seaport town of Bergen, began to furnish a simple cabinet that remained in the family for more than one hundred and fifty years. Several generations of Eeges enjoyed it and added furnishings.

The cabinet is divided into four charming rooms. The typical eighteenth-century bedroom has a black-and-white checkerboard patterned floor, imitating marble. A silk canopy supported by a headboard covers only one end of the bed. The silk quilt, embroidered in a colorful floral pattern, would have been made for a wedding, then stored in a chest and brought out only for the birth of a new baby. Upholstery on the wooden chairs and footstool is woven to look like embroidery in a popular needlework pattern known as "flame stitch."

Servants and family had their meals together in the large kitchen, where pewter plates are lined up in racks. A large open hearth in the corner, with a triangular overhang, is painted with designs that imitate Dutch tiles. In the center of the kitchen a pewter candlestick stands on a black table that has Chinese scenes painted on it in gold. In real life an Oriental lacquerware table would be considered too fancy to use in a kitchen.

Dolls' houses follow the times, as real houses do, and change as fashions change. Later generations of the Eege family modernized the living room, on the second shelf, right, in a style typical of a Bergen home in the early nineteenth century. They repainted the room with striped walls and put in new furniture. Most of it is made of cardboard. The chest, to the left in the room, was constructed of extremely light, thin wood, and the chairs are upholstered in cotton, which is cheaper than silk.

THE walls of the sitting room at the upper left were painted when the cabinet was new to imitate the walls of great seventeenth-century houses. An outdoor scene is complete with birds soaring through the sky and a sentry guarding a castle.

Bergen people have always liked to keep things in the family, so this room contains furnishings that had been inherited from earlier generations. Gilt-framed paintings hanging on the walls are protected with glass, and carved wooden chairs with high, straight backs are upholstered in silk brocade. In the course of time Bergen merchants would travel to other European countries and bring home gifts. The round tables and tea sets were given to the children as playthings, and they are more crudely made than miniature porcelain for adult collectors.

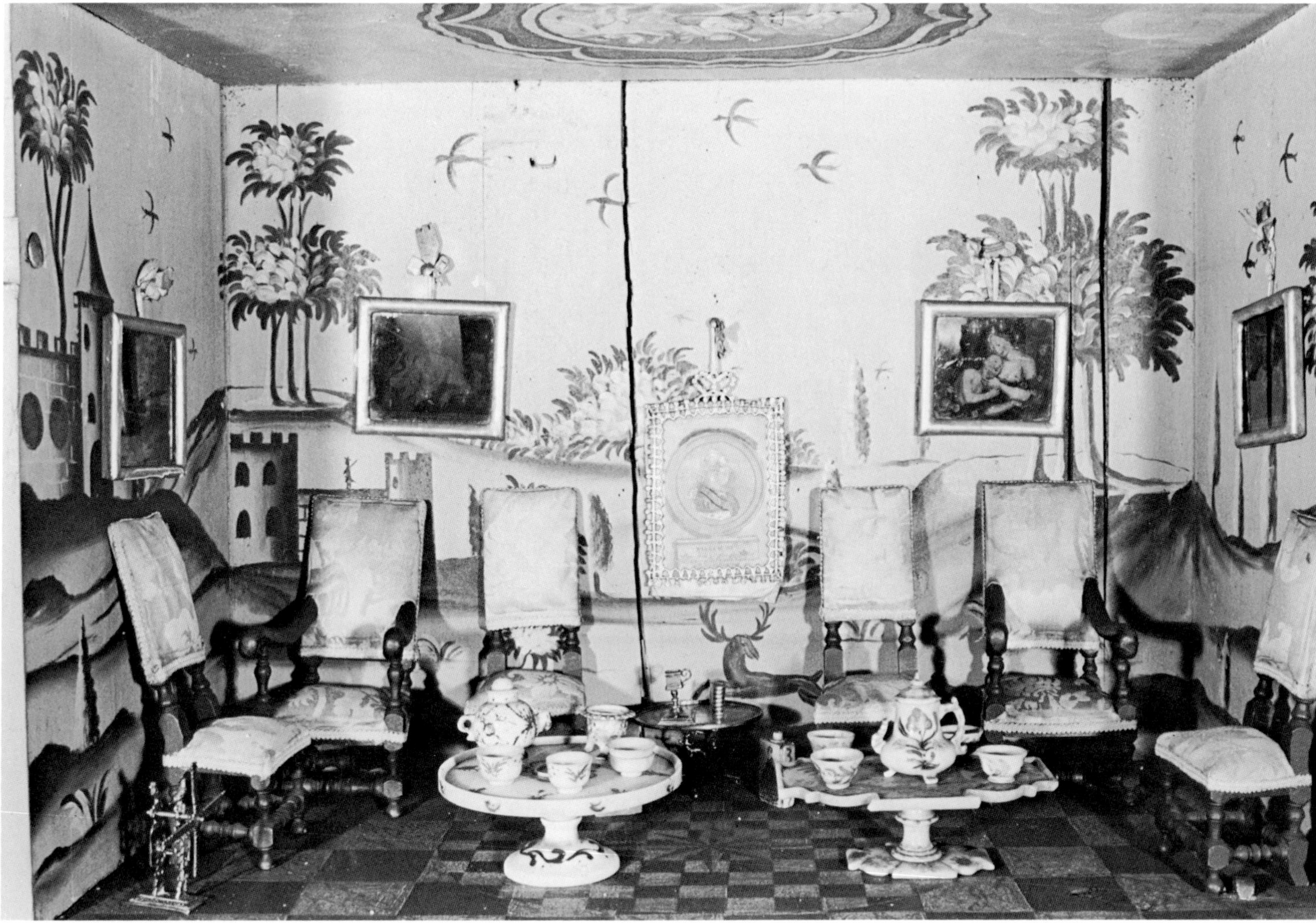

Vestlandske Kunstindustrimuseum, Bergen

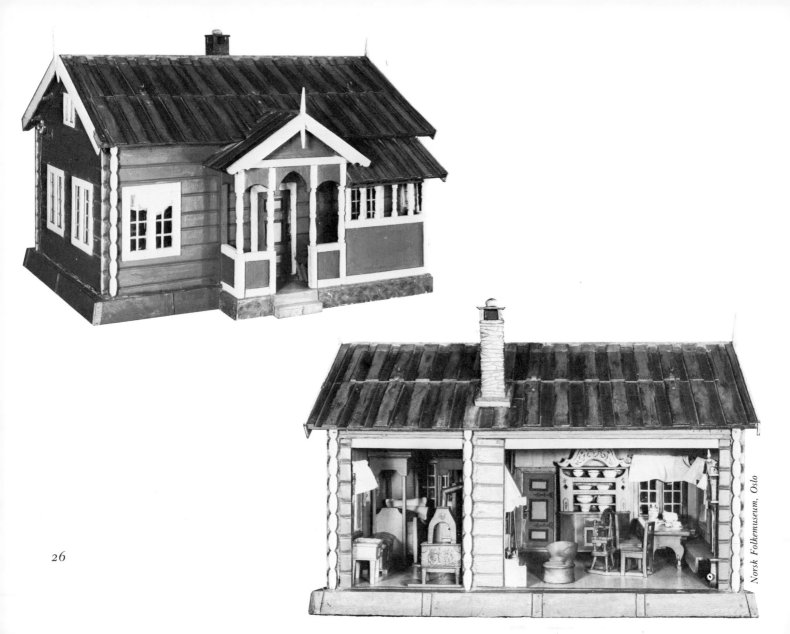

26

CHILDREN were not allowed to play with the seventeenth- and eighteenth-century cabinets of miniature treasures. But in the mid-nineteenth century a Norwegian clergyman made a simple little house for his grandchildren. It was easy to play with, as the back comes off and the roof can fold back on hinges. The style is typical of a Norwegian farmhouse that was popular in rural areas of Scandinavia for hundreds of years. It is made entirely of wood, but a real house of this type would have a roof made of thatch, or grass, laid over birch bark.

THE inside duplicates a mid-nineteenth-century tourist station, where people who traveled by horseback, stagecoach or carriage could rest and change horses. A cold, weary traveler would enter the house, walk straight to the open fireplace in the room at right and sit down on the round chair made of one big log. There was no separate kitchen or dining room in simple houses. Meals were cooked in the fireplace and served at the long table. There were few chairs; people sat on the bench while dining. The place at the end of the table where the master of a household sat was called the "high seat."

Only a well-to-do traveler could afford to sleep in the bedroom heated by an iron stove. Sheets, pillows and comforters filled with goose down would keep this traveler warm. There was also a washstand, in the foreground at left. Before the late nineteenth century most homes did not have running water. Water was usually brought from a stream or pumped from a well, or rain was collected in a cistern on the roof. It was carried inside in a pail, then kept in pitchers on washstands. Extra blankets, linens and clothes were stored in the painted chest between this washstand and the bed. Chests were the only places for storage in modest homes. Young girls would begin at an early age to put things away for their weddings in what was called a "hope chest."

There is another bedroom in the attic under the roof. However, there is no washstand, nor chest nor bed linens, in this attic room. Travelers were expected to share the beds, even if they were strangers.

27

28

FINE seventeenth-century dolls' house cabinets, made in Germany, are without legs, so they can be set on a table. The cabinet doors are usually painted to look like the stonework facades of real homes, with little windows and doors and roofs with chimneys on top. Very often these cabinets have courtyards and staircases inside.

This German cabinet represents a simple workman's home in Nuremberg. The large rectangular blocks of stone and the rounded shingles of the roof are clearly painted. The arched doorway has a little brass knocker, and there are seven windows with tiny round panes made of thin sheets of mica set into lead frames. Three open windows on the roof look out from the attic. The center one is like a large warehouse window, so goods could be hauled up on a pulley and stored in the attic. Stars on top of the window and next to the chimney were common decorations on Nuremberg homes until about 1700, when the city passed a law forbidding these decorations for fear they might fall off and hurt someone. The date 1673 on the chimney tells when the cabinet was made. A latch and tiny keyhole on the center of the facade hold the doors in place.

29

THE doors swing out, and neat curtains on the windows and a bell over the entrance can be seen. A woman stands in front of a high bed on a wooden platform, built against the wall. There are fluffy pillows and a warm comforter filled with soft goose down. The bed in the adjacent room is set into a corner alcove to save space. A large, square porcelain stove in the other corner heats this room.

The room on the ground floor to the left is the scullery, where utensils were cleaned and kitchen equipment stored. Large pewter plates line the left wall, and tankards, mugs with lids that open and close on hinges, hang in a neat row below them. Next to the scullery is the kitchen. Dinner will be cooked in the raised hooded oven in the far right corner and served on the round table. There is no sitting room nor dining room in this simple home. Extra objects that can be placed in this house are in the foreground.

Kitchens were so important they became popular as one-room dolls' houses. They were complete with every imaginable household utensil and could be used to teach little girls how to prepare food and keep things in their proper places. These miniature kitchens were first made in the seventeenth century, in the Netherlands, Germany and England. By the end of the nineteenth century most of them were manufactured in America, but they were still called "Nuremberg kitchens," after the town in Germany that for a long time was the toy center of the world.

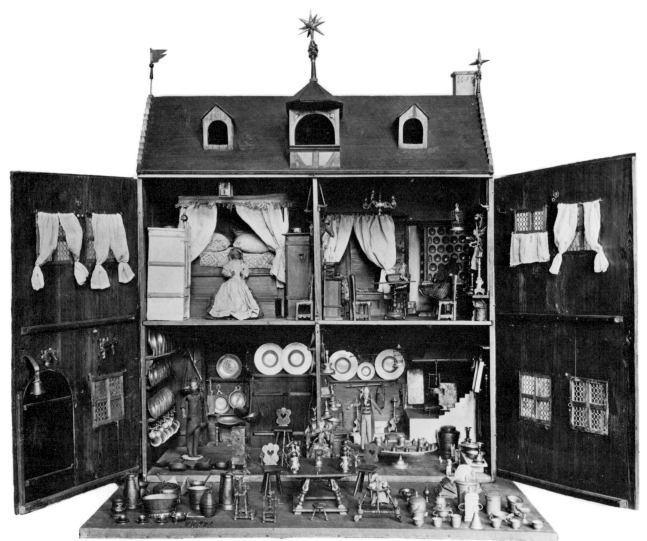

Crown Copyright, Victoria and Albert Museum,
Bethnal Green Museum of Childhood

31

Germanisches
Nationalmuseum,
Nuremberg

◆§ LUCKY little girls who played with this elaborate seventeenth-century German merchant's house could learn all there was to know about their housekeeping duties. In the top-story nursery bedroom, on the far right, a mother looks in on her children. Clothes were stored here in the tall cupboard and letters written at the desk by the windows. To the left of the nursery is a hallway, with an arched doorway that does not lead anywhere. To the left of that is a sitting room heated by a large ceramic stove. And the room on the far left is the "best kitchen," where fine pewter plates and European chinaware are displayed. There was very little Chinese porcelain in German homes, as Germany did not participate in the China trade.

Just below the "best kitchen" is the working kitchen, with a great open fireplace to cook the family's meals. Everyone dined here, as there was no separate dining room. In the sitting room on the right, four little girls wearing long dresses like their mothers' are about to have a tea party.

In the stable, on the ground level, horses stand quietly in their stalls and a sheep nibbles on stray bits of hay. Propped up in the corner are a shovel and pitchfork. A tin lantern in the middle of the ceiling lights the stable, and baskets and buckets hang on the wall ready for use.

Merchants usually had their businesses in their own homes. The room on the far right is a store that sells spices and paper. Goods were delivered to the house, unloaded in the courtyard, then taken to the shop to be counted and registered in an account book. Extra merchandise was hauled up to the attic storeroom on the pulley above the center attic window. Some spices were hung from the ceiling of the shop to dry, and others were kept in drawers. When a customer bought spices, they were weighed in the balance scale hanging from the ceiling. A metal weight would be put on one pan of the scale and the spices in the other. Six weights, in different sizes, can be seen in the left foreground. Money taken in was kept in a strongbox.

Neatly folded paper, also sold in the store, is kept on narrow open shelves along the rear wall. It would be cut to the proper size with the scissors on the table.

A SMALL boy is sweeping, and a larger-sized maid is feeding the chickens in the big courtyard in the center of the ground floor. The chicken coop is in the foreground at the left. The back wall of this courtyard is painted with an outdoor scene of a long formal garden, with another house in the distance. In real life a courtyard would be open to the sky. A tin lantern hangs from the ceiling, and brass sconces with wax candles are attached to either side of the wall. A painted staircase behind a pillar appears to lead from the garden to the floors above, but it actually goes only to the top of the first shelf. Most dolls' house staircases do not go anywhere.

Many of the furnishings in the courtyard were made in the seventeenth century and the dolls in the eighteenth century, but the coach and the animals, as well as the maid, are from the nineteenth century.

35

Museum of London

MINIATURE houses with collections of tiny treasures were especially popular among people who lived on large estates in England. They are elegant examples of English architecture, with graceful facades, outside staircases, roofs and chimneys. English families owning large country houses employed their own carpenters and cabinetmakers. Very often the dolls' house was designed by an architect, and the plans carried out by the estate carpenter with the architect supervising the construction. Or sometimes the family cabinetmaker built it and carved all the miniature furniture. Until the middle of the nineteenth century English dolls' houses were called ''baby houses''; ''baby'' was the word used for doll. Some of the ''baby houses'' were supposedly made for children, but actually young people were rarely allowed to play with them because their contents were so fragile.

The Blackett baby house, constructed about 1740, has a double flight of stairs with a dainty handrail leading from the street to the main entrance. A paneled door is surrounded by carefully carved stonework. The fanlight, or semicircular window above the door, allows daylight into the entrance hallway. Over the fanlight is a little balustrade and window topped by a pediment, or triangular space formed by the peak of the roof and the slope of its sides. Andrea Palladio, an Italian architect and scholar whose work was popular in England in the eighteenth century, incorporated classical Greek and Roman art into his architectural designs. The Palladian style was fashionable even for dolls' houses.

The front panels of the Blackett house unlock and swing open on hinges to reveal four beautiful rooms. The windows slide up and down as real windows do, and the curtains can be raised and lowered with cords that wind around knobs to hold them in place. These are the original curtains. Usually such fragile furnishings would have worn out in the course of two and a half centuries.

In a real house the kitchen would be on the ground floor near a service entrance, so servants could carry in food without disturbing the family. But here the kitchen is at the right of the entrance hall. Among the utensils is a roasting jack, a metal

37

device with weights and chains, which had to be wound up and then would turn the spit slowly so the meat could cook evenly on all sides.

The furniture and dolls in the Blackett baby house are in almost perfect proportion to each other and to the house itself. However, the candlesticks in the bedroom seem a bit large for the little chest of drawers with its tiny brass handles. The white pitcher and basin were used for people to wash themselves. For bathing a metal tub would be brought out and filled with water.

The Chinese wallpaper on the second floor has a pattern of flowers. The idea of decorating walls with painted paper originated in China. At first all wallpaper was hand painted and was imported from the Far East. Then Europeans began

to make their own hand-painted paper; later they began to print the patterns for mass production.

⊷ THE entrance hall leads into the dining room, where hand-painted paper with scenes of Italian ruins decorates the walls. Pompeii, an ancient Roman city near Naples that was covered with volcanic ash when Mt. Vesuvius erupted in A.D. 79, had been recently discovered, and having an interest in archaeology and ancient Greek and Roman temples became very fashionable.

The drop-leaf table in this dining room has leaves that can be raised to make the table bigger. There is a cloth rug on the floor; most eighteenth-century baby houses had painted floors.

39

THIS three-story baby house was made for a girl named Sarah around 1730. When she married an English nobleman she took it with her to Uppark, the country estate that was their home. Several generations of children were allowed to play with it. Nevertheless, after two hundred and fifty years it still has all of its original furnishings, including a tiny ivory set of dominoes in a wooden box. This is unusual, for most dolls' houses have later additions, as objects got lost or broken or else were replaced because the owners felt they had gone out of style.

A shield with the family's coat of arms is painted in the center of the pediment. A graceful statue stands on a base at the peak of the roof, and six others are poised on the balustrade.

Each of the nine rooms opens separately. They are all furnished in a popular style named after Queen Anne, who ruled England from 1702 until 1714.

In the entrance hall, on the first level, a teapot stands on a gate-legged table, one that has side leaves that can be folded down so the table can be made smaller, to save space. Tea was first brought to Europe from China in Dutch ships in the seventeenth century. The English people liked it so much that it became their most important beverage, and teatime, in the late afternoon, became a daily social event.

In the dining room, in the center, framed oil paintings of outdoor scenes hang high on the painted, paneled wall. A well-dressed lady and gentleman admire the family silver, which was created by silversmiths identifiable by their hallmarks. Glassware is lined up on a small table with an imitation marble top. This fine glassware is from the workshops of Waterford, Ireland, where exquisite crystal is still being made and exported all over the world. The gate-legged table and the chairs in this dining room have cabriole legs, which turn outward. Cabriole legs were typical of the Queen Anne furniture style.

The grand beds in the four bedrooms have flaring silk curtains. In the second-floor bedroom, twin babies lie in a cradle under the watchful eye of a nursemaid. At the far left is the sitting room, where people are chatting over tea.

42

Most English baby houses are about three feet tall; the Tate house, made about 1760, is more than five feet tall. It has an elegant Palladian facade, and a double flight of stairs encloses the checkered marble flooring that leads to the arched doorway of a ground-level entrance. The pantry and kitchen would be reached through this entrance and would be used mostly by servants. Round windows are set into the brick wall on either side. A symmetrical and balanced design is typical of Palladian architecture.

Stonework covers most of the wall on the ground floor and the projecting corners of the building all the way up to the roof. The rest of the house is brickwork. Pediments over the doorway at the main entrance, over the upper row of windows and over the arched window on the second story are Palladian features. All the windows can be raised and lowered. A skylight in the center of the roof admits light to the central staircase from above.

PAPER with big birds, butterflies and flowers covers the walls of rooms in an English cabinet that was owned by a wealthy physician. It was made in about 1835, seventy-five years after the Tate house, and the rooms are furnished in the spacious, comfortable manner of large homes of the period.

Women dressed in beautiful clothes made by the wife and daughter of the owner of the dolls' house are gathered in the bedroom. When she goes out, one of these stylish ladies will wear the tiny gloves on the stool at the foot of the bed and carry the folded parasol that leans against the wall at the right, next to the dressing table. Ladies always wore hats and gloves and carried parasols in public. To the left in this room is a washstand and towel rack. Patterned cloth rugs cover the floors.

In another part of the physician's cabinet a doll family is gathered in the sitting room, or parlor, which is also called the drawing room because people withdrew there from the dining room after dinner. Nowadays it is usually called the living room. The fireplace has a grate for burning coal, which was cheaper and burned longer than wood. Miniature photographs of members of the family look down from the wall. The daguerreotype, the first practical method of photography, was invented about the time this cabinet was built, and it was fashionable to have one's picture taken.

A painting in an ornate frame covers the wall over the mantel. The two sofas, covered with striped silk, are in the Empire style, named after the French style created for the emperor Napoleon. Other chairs, with tall, straight backs, are carved in an openwork design that was popular in the nineteenth century.

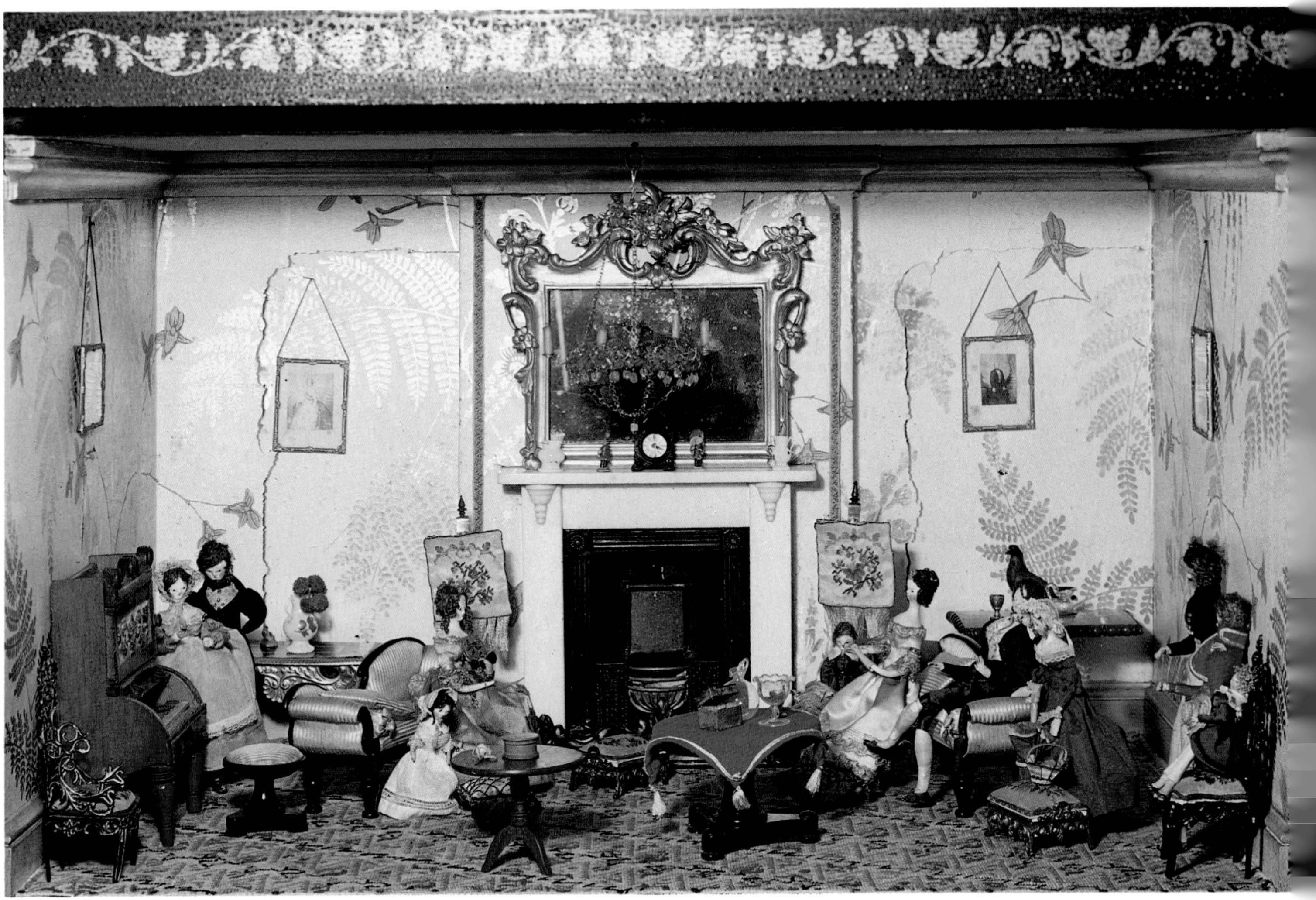

A LOVELY nine-room dolls' house was made in about 1735 for the family that built an estate known as Nostell Priory. The architect for the estate house is thought to have also designed the dolls' house; and the famous cabinetmaker Thomas Chippendale lived in the neighborhood and is thought to have taken part in it. The Palladian-style facade can be lifted off in two sections.

In the kitchen, on the first level, three arched brick ovens are built into the tiled wall. The wide entrance hall is covered with panels of natural wood. A broad staircase goes nowhere.

In the first-floor sitting room, also wood paneled, is a large landscape painting that covers the wall over the fireplace. The bedroom, on the second level, has crimson velvet curtains; the ones in the room at top right are made of flowered chintz. The tiny furniture is exquisitely carved; most of it is made of mahogany, a fine dark wood.

The room on the second level at right has an elaborate marble fireplace of classical design, adapted from ancient Greek and Roman temple motifs. A bust, or tiny sculptured portrait head, sits on the mantel and is framed by flowing painted patterns. The walls are covered with romantic landscapes. They were made from engraved pictures, imported from France, that were cut out and hand painted. Almost all of the furnishings in the Nostell Priory baby house are original.

੬§ "DINGLEY HALL" was made in 1874 for two English schoolboys, Laurence and Isaac Currie, and most of the dolls that occupy it are male. It has thirteen elegant rooms and an entrance hall where visitors are greeted by a statue of an ancient Greek goddess. A carpeted staircase with a brass rod on each step to hold the carpet in place leads to the second story, where miniature copies of ancient Greek vases are lined up behind a balustrade.

Hanging on the wall on the second story are two plaques, one with miniature arms of the Middle Ages and the other with an arrangement of small musical instruments. There is a piano on the floor above, so the Currie boys must have been interested in music as well as medieval knights.

51

In the late nineteenth century it was fashionable in large English houses to have billiard rooms and smoking rooms for the men. When there was a large staff of servants, it would be a butler's duty to make certain that the cloth on the billiard table was brushed and pressed. Miss Miles's dolls' house has a billiard table with overhanging electric lights. On the desk is an old-fashioned upright telephone with a receiver that dangles from a hook next to the mouthpiece. Electricity and the telephone were recent inventions. In case the electricity went out, as it often did, candles were always handy. Horse racing pictures on the wall add to the masculine character of the room. One of the men is holding a copy of *The Illustrated London News*, a weekly magazine that is still popular in England.

MISS MILES'S house was made by a commercial firm in 1890. By the late nineteenth century a large variety of simple dolls' houses that were strongly constructed for children to play with could be bought ready-made. Some even came already furnished with factory-made objects. Miss Miles's original dolls' house had three stories with eight rooms. The billiard room was part of an addition added to the dolls' house at a later time, just as additions are made to enlarge real houses.

The new addition also includes an artist's studio in the attic, where a skylight lets in the daylight, making this a bright place in which to paint. When the model becomes weary of posing for her portrait, she can rest on the folding camp-stool. The dangling skeleton is used by the artist to study anatomy. Pictures that he has already finished are hanging on the wall.

55

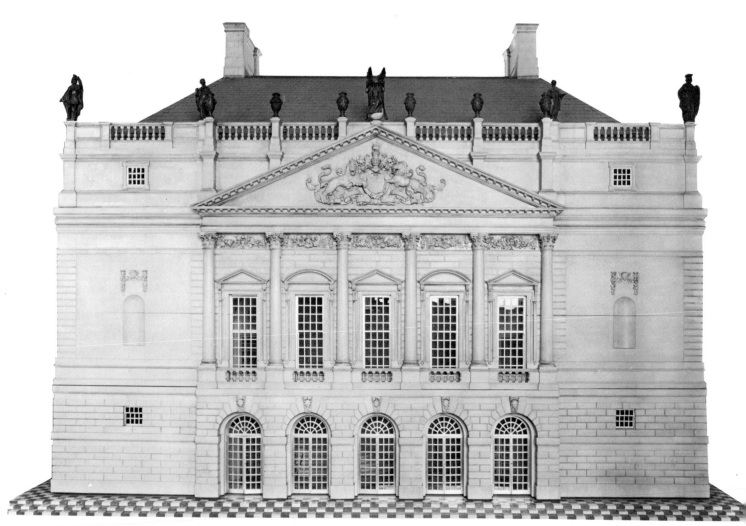

ONE of the world's largest dolls' houses was designed for Her Majesty Queen Mary, grandmother of Queen Elizabeth II. It is about eight and a half feet long by five feet wide, and its contents are in the standard scale of one twelfth actual size. As a child, Queen Mary loved to play with dolls' houses. Then in 1924 she was presented with a model royal residence, designed by the architect Sir Edwin Lutyens. It was patterned after great English country houses in the Renaissance style, which adapted features of ancient Roman buildings. The outside has classical columns framing tall windows that open onto little balconies. On the ground floor there are five arched doors with rectangular panes of glass and semicircular fanlights. The royal coat of arms of the House of Windsor fills the center of the pediment, and lead statues and vases decorate the parapet over the attic.

THE outer walls can be raised by means of an electrical device that operates on the same principal as an elevator. When a button is pressed, it starts a motor that sets off a pulley that works on a fishing line. There are also two passenger elevators inside. This mansion is equipped with tiny electric lights that are turned off and on with a switch, and electrical appliances such as a vacuum cleaner and iron. There is even a kitchen scale, a knife sharpener and a sewing machine operated by a foot treadle.

Underneath one side of the house is a garden. On the other side is a garage where the royal automobiles are parked. These include 1923 and 1924 models of a Lanchester, a Vauxhall, a Rolls-Royce, a Sunbeam, two Daimlers and a Rudge motorcycle six and three quarters inches long with a sidecar and a gasoline engine that works. A gas pump and everything needed to repair a car are in the garage, and there is even a fire cart with ladders on hand in case of emergency. Bicycles and prams for infant princes and princesses are also stored here.

Everything a royal residence might have, from basement to attic, is in this royal dolls' house. There are golf clubs in leather bags for the king's recreation. Each object was made to order by a leading craftsman; even the bed linens were specially woven. Bottles of wine only an inch high were made to serve at royal dinners, and tiny keys, almost too small to turn, open all the doors.

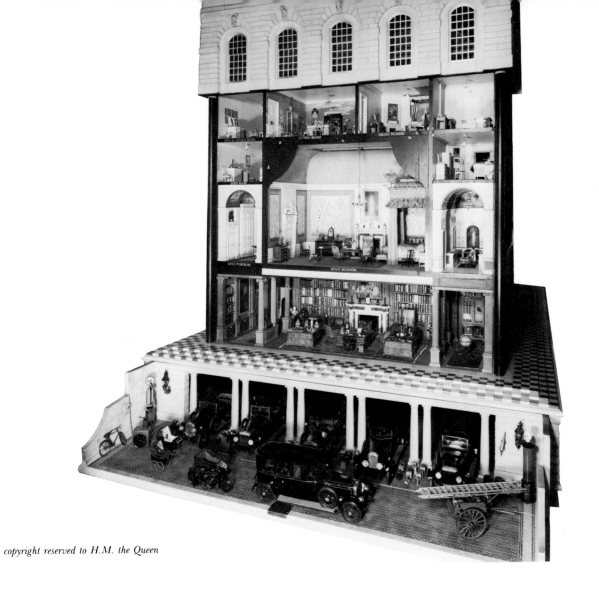

59

MODELS of knights in medieval armor guard the entrance hall, which has a floor with a checkerboard pattern imitating blue and white marble. A painting of Windsor Castle, the royal residence where this huge dolls' house is located, hangs over the table. Next to it is a tall female statue and a grandfather clock.

THE vaulted ceiling of King George's bathroom is hand painted. The floor is white marble, and the bathtub and double washbasin are made of green marble imported from Africa. Silver taps control the flow of hot and cold water; the waste water empties into a tank in the basement.

In the royal library, portraits of Queen Elizabeth I and King Henry VIII hang on walls paneled in Italian walnut. Near the walnut columns is a world globe so the king could keep a finger on the vast British Empire, and a model of his yacht, the *Royal George.* The fireplace is made of lapis lazuli, a semiprecious stone. About seven hundred drawings are stored in the library cabinets, and the shelves hold two hundred books bound in fine leather, with their titles embossed in gold. Each is handwritten and autographed by a famous author of the day, including Rudyard Kipling and Somerset Maugham.

Messages to the king from various departments of the British government are kept in boxes on the leather-topped desk. And in case of fire or theft a householder's insurance policy is tucked away in this library. There is also a phonograph with records only an inch in diameter, and a safe with a lock and key for the crown jewels. The library carpet is woven in a Persian design, and the designs on the ceiling are hand painted.

ONE summer day in 1907 a three-year-old girl named Guendolen was playing in the garden of her home in Ireland when she saw one of the little fairies who dance around the old sycamore tree every night in the moonlight. Guendolen asked her father to build a house for the fairy, whom they named Titania (the queen of the fairies in Shakespeare's play *A Midsummer Night's Dream*). Guendolen's father, Sir Nevile Wilkinson, an English nobleman who was a painter and the author of several children's stories about fairies, drew up plans for a palace that would befit Titania's royal fairy family.

With a team of outstanding artists and craftsmen he spent the next fifteen years constructing and furnishing a spectacular dolls' house that was officially opened with a golden key in 1922 by Queen Mary of England. *The Illustrated London News* called it "the most wonderful dolls' house ever built."

Entering Titania's Palace is like entering a dream world. There are seventeen rooms enclosing a garden said to be the same garden where the pumpkin grew that became Cinderella's horse-drawn coach. The palace is furnished with miniature antiques and precious treasures that Sir Nevile had been collecting for years. He also had copies made of the finest furniture, in ideal dolls' house scale of an inch to a foot. There are three thousand objects in all.

THE Fairy Queen receives her guests in the Hall of the Guilds. The walls are painted in tiny dots of watercolor that look like mosaic work, a technique developed by Sir Nevile. Winged maidens in framed tapestries hold the royal coat of arms and shields with emblems of Florentine craftsmen's guilds. Sir Nevile also designed the ceiling inlaid with seashells, and the colorful silk banners embroidered with heraldic symbols. The Renaissance miniature cannon in the foreground is attributed to Michael Mann of Nuremburg.

In the background two sixteenth-century bronze horses proudly prance on majestic stands on either side of the entrance to the throne room, where Titania in her pearl-studded royal crown holds court seated on the peacock throne.

DANCES and celebrations were held in the Hall of the Fairy Kiss, where the floor is made of two thousand pieces of inlaid wood, and views of blossoming trees in the garden can be seen through the glass windows. A mosaic frieze runs around the room at the top of the walls, and a gold chandelier with an electric light bulb hangs from the center of the elaborately patterned ceiling. The entire palace is lit by electricity. Two Chinese Ming porcelain vases are displayed on stands, and enclosed in chains is the royal sleigh. It is said that Santa Claus borrows this sleigh every year at Christmastime, and Prince Zephyr and Prince Noel, Titania's two older boys, help Santa carry his sacks of gifts.

There are numerous miniature statues in the Hall of the Fairy Kiss. A tiny gold Hindu god from India is enclosed in a silver-framed glass case resting on ivory elephants, and three Italian Renaissance bronze figures are poised on the banister of the broad walnut staircase leading to the musicians' gallery. Hanging near the top of the staircase is a portrait of Queen Mary.

Wooden lions stand on either side of the green-marble fireplace. The silk-embroidered banner above it bears Titania's butterfly symbol, and her motto, NIHIL SINE LABORE, Latin for "Nothing Without Work." In the middle of the room is a chest with the insignias of the highest order of Fairyland, honors bestowed only on those who prove themselves worthy by living up to Titania's motto.

68

To pass from the Hall of the Fairy Kiss to the Queen's private chapel guests can walk through a silver door; fairies can fly through windows.

The chapel has a floor of Carrara marble, and a ceiling with religious motifs in the Byzantine style. The altar screen was copied from a madonna in a painting of the Assumption. The books on the altar are a beautifully illustrated French Book of Hours, dated 1450; the complete New Testament; and a leather-bound volume clasped in gold of extracts from the Bible. An organ in a magnificent wooden frame actually can be played by blowing through the bellows and pressing the keys with matchsticks.

The chapel is one of four rooms in the palace that are two stories tall.

A secret panel in the wall of the chapel can be opened to transport the Fairy Queen to her private boudoir, decorated in the Sheraton style. The floor of this magnificent room is inlaid with mother-of-pearl and a variety of fine woods. In her boudoir, Titania can be alone and perhaps rest in the comfortable upholstered chair in front of the fireplace. The smaller round table holds a silver teapot, but fairies do not drink tea nor require food, as they, like the gods, live on nectar and on the fragrance of fruit. And they bathe in dewdrops that collect on rose petals, so there is no running water in the palace. If Titania gets industrious she can spin thread on the ivory spinning wheel. Sleeping Beauty is said to have pricked her finger on the spindle of this spinning wheel.

In the glass case on the semicircular commode is a drop of rock crystal, which symbolizes the first tears of a newborn baby. The commode itself, which is five and a half inches wide and has a beautiful veneered surface, was signed by the cabinetmaker A. Dunn and Company, of Dublin, and dated 1922. The Fairy Queen keeps her paintbrushes in the rectangular worktable so they are easily available if an artistic mood strikes. The tiny stationery on which she writes her letters bears her monogram.

FRIENDS who call on the royal family are received in the spacious private entrance hall. As they enter, visitors may sign the guest book located on an elaborate stand set with opals and supported by a gilt-legged table. It has been signed by such famous people as Queen Mary, the movie stars Shirley Temple and Charlie Chaplin and the poet W. B. Yeats. A large plate-glass window in the background provides a wonderful view of the garden. Potted plants in front of the window hold flowers that are always in bloom. A pram for the infant princes and princesses, and a bicycle for the older children, are parked in the foreground, ready for use. Titania and Oberon have four daughters and three sons.

The chandelier can hold candles in case the electric lights should go out. A double staircase with mosaic pictures and potted plants on the landing leads to the royal bedchamber on the floor above.

IVORY cupids and carved and painted figures and royal symbols adorn the Renaissance-style four-poster bed. The monogram embroidered on the pristine white coverlet is a T with a royal crown. There are ivory statues on the mantelpiece. The backs of the red lacquer chairs are painted with figures of a fairy and a peacock. The queen's treasures, like her tiny diamond and ruby rings and a gold thimble, are kept in her golden jewel box. Some of the miniature chinaware was a gift from Queen Mary.

Legoland A/S

◆§ TINY Chinese lions of malachite guard the spectacular ebony-and-ivory throne, with its two sixteenth-century Italian gold figures perched on the arms. The back of the throne is adorned with a peacock, enhanced with diamonds, rubies, emeralds and sapphires, perching on a pearl. The brooch the peacock was made from was originally worn by Empress Eugénie of France. (A peacock is actually prince consort Oberon's symbol; Titania's symbol is a butterfly.) And the beautiful mosaic ceiling of this room bears the names of famous authors of fairy tales.

Legoland A/S
Photograph by Hanne Richter

76

꿍 SINCE Colonial days the city of Philadelphia, Pennsylvania, has been known for its beautiful architecture and excellent cabinetmakers. A dolls' house made in Philadelphia around 1810 for a family named Dickey resembles a real Philadelphia home of the period. It is carved and painted to look like stonework, with a plain trim going all the way around between the stories. The front of the house opens on hinges and can be locked shut. The keyholes have Green Tree fire marks over them. These emblems were put on a house by the company that insured it. Each insurance company had its own fire department, which would put out a fire only if the owner of the house had an insurance policy with that company. It was Benjamin Franklin, who lived in Philadelphia, who started the first fire company in America.

Three steps in front lead up to a paneled wooden door with a simple fanlight and brass keyhole. The surface of the hipped roof—a roof flat on top and sloping on all four sides—represents overlapping shingles. Two brick chimneys are connected to the fireplaces in the rooms beneath. Between the chimneys is a balustrade, commonly called a "captain's walk."

Most early American dolls' houses are box-like and symmetrical, but one that was made in New York around 1840 by Reverend Philip Brett for the children in his family has an irregular floor plan. The central section is two stories high, with a false attic that has a window with shutters. Wings on either side are only one story high. A brick fence with an iron gate encloses a lawn and flower garden; and a porch at left serves as another entrance. Front porches were common on Victorian homes. In summertime they became a kind of extra living room where people gathered. Behind the house is an outdoor toilet, or outhouse, which was necessary before there was indoor plumbing.

The floors are covered with embroidered and hooked rugs, and in the upstairs bedroom one can sit on a rocking chair, another of Benjamin Franklin's innovations. The doll family can gather in the drawing room and play music on the piano and harp, reading notes from the song-book on the music stand.

Rooms where the family gathered, on the ground floor, all look out on the garden in the back of the house. To get a breath of fresh air one could walk into the garden by passing through the two French doors, with fanlights over them, in the living room.

There are only four rooms, although the house seems larger because the rooms are so spacious and comfortable looking. And even though it was played with by four generations of Brett children, the original dolls and much of the original furniture remain.

In Salem, Massachusetts, another town on the Atlantic coast, two little girls named Mamie and Millie received a dolls' house built by their father, Benjamin Chamberlain, as a Christmas gift in 1883. Mr. Chamberlain was a silversmith, and he engraved the girls' names on a tiny silver plaque on the front door. The house is a sturdy structure, made of wood that was carved and then stained. There is carved decoration over the porches, the front door and the windows, and on the graceful cupola. The facade slides off in two sections, one on either side of the main entranceway. There are bay windows above the kitchen wing, on the opposite side of the house and also over the front porch. Bay windows project beyond the wall to admit extra daylight, add extra space and provide a cozy little area within a room.

As a silversmith, Mr. Chamberlain was skillful at working metals. He made the gilded metal railings for the bay windows, the cupola and the kitchen wing.

Among the interesting objects in the house are an old-fashioned tennis racquet and a thermometer outside the porch. Some pieces of furniture were gifts from friends who had traveled in Europe. There is actually a surplus of furnishings in the house, but a cluttered interior was fashionable in the Victorian period. This period was named after the queen who ruled England from 1837 until 1901. All the curtains and linens were made by Mamie and Millie's mother. Their father made the sterling silver tea service.

81

A Baltimore carpenter made a dolls' house and presented it to Fanny Hayes, daughter of President Rutherford B. Hayes, in 1878. She and her little brother, Scott, played with it when they lived in the White House. It is three stories high and has a mansard roof, with very slight slopes on all four sides and steeper slopes below that. Dormers, windows projecting from the sloping roof, admit light and air into the attic, where servants usually had their living quarters in a nineteenth-century home. The rest of the attic space would be used for storage. The four narrow chimneys and belvedere, or lookout tower, make the roof seem even taller. A trim of fancy ornament, commonly called "gingerbread," decorates the edges of the roof. Gingerbread ornament could be cut out with a saw by a carpenter. It was highly popular on Victorian houses because it was an attractive, yet inexpensive, form of decoration for a wooden house. There is also carved trimming over the door and windows and on the little balconies.

Victorian architecture incorporated all periods of the past. Gingerbread ornament and windows with patterned glass were inspired by arches and spires on the Gothic cathedrals of medieval times.

Rutherford B. Hayes Presidential Center

THERE is a good deal of gingerbread and also several stained-glass windows on the house that a cabinetmaker built in 1893 for Fred Vogel of Milwaukee, Wisconsin. Stained glass was ordered from Europe by the square yard before American craftsmen began making it. There are six plaster female heads and other ornaments in the corners and rims around the rooms.

The interior is decorated in the style of a comfortable home of a German-American family in the late nineteenth century. The sturdy cherrywood furniture was imported from Germany when the house was new, and much of it still remains, as do the original dolls.

There are plenty of toys for the children to play with, including a dolls' dolls' house with a stable full of horses. In the kitchen, at the lower left, are two objects that were common in homes of the period—a metal milk pail and a little seat made from a wooden butter churn.

The house also opens from the side to give a good view of the staircase running from bottom to top.

Milwaukee Public Museum

85

86

A TWO-STORY brick house is furnished in the style of a New Jersey home of the late nineteenth century. It has large rooms with high ceilings, which were fashionable in Victorian times although chilly in winter. A fireplace or stove in each room kept the family as warm as possible in the days before homes would have central warm-air furnaces. Rooms would be lit by oil lamps and by chandeliers that burned gas piped into the home.

Lace curtains and iron furniture were popular at this time. There is an iron bed in the bedroom, and an iron stand holds a sewing machine that was propelled by a foot treadle, as there was no electricity. On a bench in the kitchen is a washtub with a washboard to scrub the clothes. Everything had to be laundered by hand. Hot water had to be heated in a kettle on the gas range, or in a hot-water tank hooked up to it. Gas ranges began to take the place of wood or coal stoves of earlier days.

A large family and several servants live in this house. By the late nineteenth century small dolls for dolls' houses no longer had to be made by hand with handsewn clothes. Just as sets of furniture were available in stores, dolls' house dolls could be bought in sets, already dressed.

The plumbing in the bathroom, with sink, shower and toilet with a pull-chain flush, was a twentieth-century addition to the house. In the late nineteenth century some upper-class homes had bathrooms, but plumbing and fixtures were still very expensive.

By the end of the nineteenth century most dolls' houses were factory made. The rooms pictured here are in a commercial house that was bought for a child named Altadena in 1895. Some of the rooms still have their original furnishings. When Altadena grew up and had a little girl who played with the house, new objects were added.

Solid-colored walls had come into fashion, and the walls of the sitting room on the first floor are painted. The patterned rug is embroidered with wool thread on canvas, in the petit-point stitch. A mirror in a fancy frame hangs over the fireplace, and a crystal chandelier with light bulbs drops from the ceiling. Candles in candlesticks and in wall brackets give extra light. Even after houses were wired for electricity, candles remained popular. They were useful in case the electricity failed, as it often did, and they were used for decorations to give soft light, especially while dining. Other interesting objects in the room are the fine porcelain, a tiny deck of cards on the round table in the foreground and a violin on the wingback chair in the left corner. Tea will soon be poured at a small round tea table near the fireplace. When the logs are burning, a firescreen, just to the left of the fireplace, can diffuse the heat so that people sitting near the fire will not feel overheated.

89

FAMOUS artists created miniature works of art the size of postage stamps for a grown-up's dolls' house that was made for Miss Carrie Stettheimer in the 1920s. She and her mother and sisters, Florine, a painter, and Ettie, a poet, lived in New York and had a great many interesting friends. The dolls' house reflects the social life of this fascinating family during the period between the two World Wars, in the great city of New York. It has rooms on all four sides and is furnished with sturdy, simple furniture in a new style of the time—"modern."

Like the family's real house, it is set up for frequent entertaining. It also has the newest conveniences. These include an elevator and full bathroom with a scale for the ladies to watch their weight, as it had become fashionable to be thin. There is also a wooden icebox, which held the large cakes of ice that would be delivered to homes each day by men driving wagons pulled by horses. Housewives put signs in their windows with numbers to tell the iceman the size of blocks needed that day.

᪥ Two famous sculptors made miniature statues that stand on the terrace outside the ballroom. On the left is a mother and child, in bronze, by William Zorach. The statue of the Roman goddess Venus was carved in white alabaster, a very fine stone, by Gaston Lachaise. When the French doors to the terrace are open, paintings by Claggett Wilson, at the left, and Carl Sprinchorn, over the fireplace, can be seen in the ballroom.

◄§ THE ballroom is a miniature art gallery. A grand piano is set up under a balcony for musicians playing string instruments, and the fireplace offers a cheery note on a cold winter evening. Paintings hanging on the wall include works by Alexander Archipenko, on the upper left, and Louis Bouché, in the middle row of pictures at the far right. The most famous painting, to the right of the fireplace, is a tiny copy of "Nude Descending a Staircase," by Marcel Duchamp, which created a sensation when it was exhibited in New York in 1913.

Dolls' houses that are being made today reflect the way we live in an age when space is limited and people are busy, so homes have to be simple, with every square foot of space carefully planned. In 1976 an architect, Ira Greenberg, designed a modern house for *Woman's Day* magazine that was put together in sections. The architect's diagrams for constructing a house like this were included in an instruction booklet that could be ordered from the magazine.

The house is set on a flat base, and includes a garage for the family automobile and a deck for dining outdoors in good weather. Little children can play with it because it is only two feet high, and the roof pieces and the second-story bedroom lift off so every room can be easily reached.

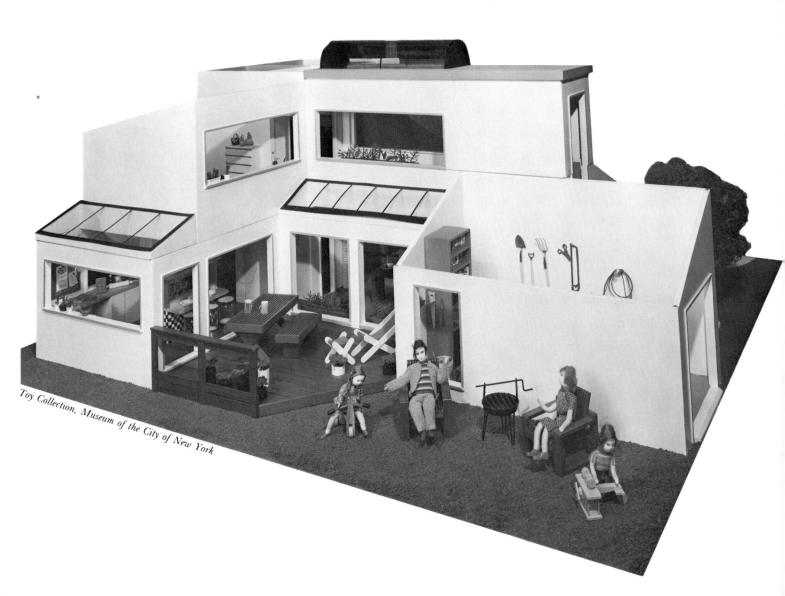

MANY of the furnishings are made of ordinary household materials. The walls are covered with gift-wrapping paper, and the floor in the kitchen is made of black tape cut into squares and arranged in a checkerboard pattern. On other floors tape was cut and laid down in patterns and then shellacked to look like parquet, or inlaid wood flooring. Felt-tipped pens, attached to wooden bases with springs, make reading lamps for the wall in the master bedroom.

The oven door is a lid from a plastic box. Water faucets are screws and bent nails, and stools are pillboxes. Paper clips are used for legs of a seat, and painted thimbles become flowerpots. A garbage can is a plastic cup covered with aluminum foil; the cover is cardboard, with staples for handles. Beads form knobs to pull open cupboard doors. Candles are matchsticks dipped in wax. Bottlecaps and caps from toothpaste tubes make lampshades. The bedspread is a kerchief, and another kerchief is mounted on bristol board and covered with vinyl to serve as a rug. Ping-Pong balls cut in half are used as lampshades, and the shower head is a pushpin mounted on a metal washer.

Dolls' houses have followed the times and changed as fashions change, reflecting the development of different life-styles for three centuries. These little houses that preserve history in a rapidly changing world have taken their place as art treasures in museums. Dolls' houses are enjoyed by everyone, from nursery to old age. It is no wonder they have become one of the world's most popular hobbies.

Toy Collection, Museum of the City of New York

Index

Page numbers in *italics* refer to illustrations.